The Lost
Deep Thoughts

By Jack Handey

Don't Fight
The Deepness

Library of Congress Cataloging-in-Publication Data

Handey, Jack.
        The lost deep thoughts : don't fight the deepness / by Jack Handey — 1st ed.
            p. cm.
        ISBN 0-7868-8305-7
        I. Title
PN6162.H276 1998
818'.5402 — dc21   98-23873
                                                    CIP

Book Design by Spinning Egg Design Group, Inc.
First Edition

10 9 8 7 6 5 4

To Beverly Marble, My Mom

Special Thanks to:
Kit Boss and Murray Smith
Kelly Cannon
Lucinda Cruse
Spike Feresten
John Fortenberry
Tom Gammill and Sandy Gillis
Megan Harrell
Byron and Theresa Laursen
Patrick Marble
Dave and Susan McIntyre
William, Ben and Jesse Novak
Max Pross and Mira Velimirovic´
...and most especially, Marta Chavez Handey

Photo Credits:
"Beach Feet," "Pugs," "Barn Cat" and "Tree Roots" by John Fortenberry; "Wet Rocks," "Shore Birds" and "Swimming Ducks" by Dave McIntyre; "Night Fern," "Wading Bird" and "Sunset Palm" by Bererly Marble; "Gas Pump" by Rick Newhouse; All other photos by Marta and Jack Handey

If you lose your job, your marriage and your mind all in one week, try to lose your mind first, because then the other stuff won't matter that much.

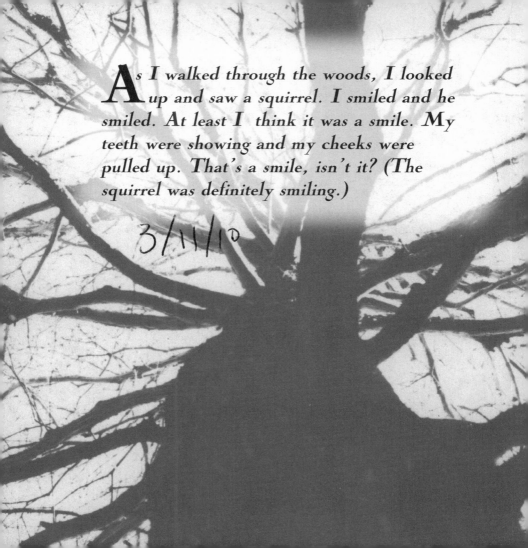

As I walked through the woods, I looked up and saw a squirrel. I smiled and he smiled. At least I think it was a smile. My teeth were showing and my cheeks were pulled up. That's a smile, isn't it? (The squirrel was definitely smiling.)

3/11/10

Probably the saddest thing you'll ever see
is a mosquito sucking on a mummy.
Forget it, little friend.

Instead of a trap door, what about an area of the floor that just shoots up real quick and smashes the guy against the ceiling?

I hope I never do anything to bring shame on myself, my family or my other family.

When I think of all the arguments Marta and I have had, I realize how silly most of them were. And it makes me wonder why she wanted to argue over such stupid things. I think I'll go ask her.

If you think a weakness can be turned into a strength, I hate to tell you this, but that's another weakness.

There is one question that probably drives just about every vampire crazy: "Oh, do you know Dracula?"

Before a mad scientist goes mad, there's probably a time when he's only partially mad. And this is the time when he's going to throw his best parties.

One good thing about hell, at least, is you can probably pee wherever you want to.

For me, the worst thing about having King Kong walk down your street is that kids could look up and see the giant genitalia.

Many people don't realize that playing dead can help not only with bears, but also at important business meetings.

The weirdest thing about going to the store and seeing a jar of pickles with your picture on it is not that your picture is on the jar. It's that the store manager won't give you the pickles for free, and doesn't even think the picture looks like you.

There's a world that we know nothing about, that we can only imagine. And that is the world of books.

If you're ever giving a speech, when you start out, act nervous and get mixed up a little bit. Then, as you go along, get better and better. Then, at the end, give off a white, glowing light and have rays shoot out of you.

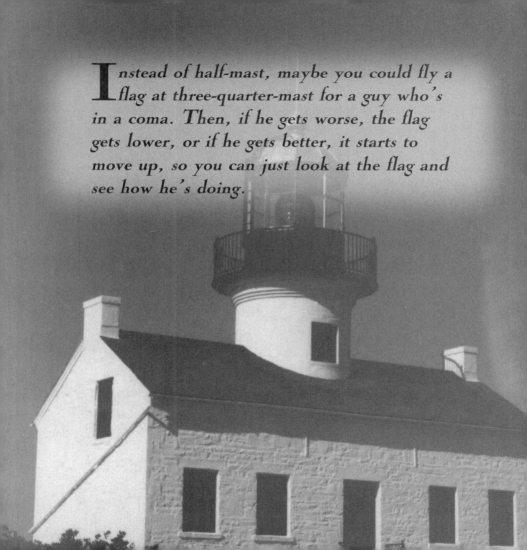

Instead of half-mast, maybe you could fly a flag at three-quarter-mast for a guy who's in a coma. Then, if he gets worse, the flag gets lower, or if he gets better, it starts to move up, so you can just look at the flag and see how he's doing.

People need to realize that every time they talk about how "fragile" our planet is, it's just like asking outer-space aliens to come invade us.

Basically, this is the way the economy works: I do a service for you, and you pay me, even if you claim you didn't want the service and that I "ruined" something of yours.

Instead of a regular arm, Carl had been born with a pigeon's wing. The odd thing was, all through his life, no one had ever laughed at his wing -- not even the mean kids at school. Then one day he realized why: He looked in the mirror and saw that HE WAS A PIGEON! He shit right there, as he often did, wherever he was.

One bad thing about Lassie, she was always warning you about something. Let me be surprised for a change.

When I shake hands with a man, the first thing I do is look him right in the eye. Then I start poking my hand around in the air, pretending like I can't find his hand. Then, if the guy's still there, I finally shake it.

What would annoy me if a space visitor ever came to our planet would be if he kept talking about things in "his world." Your world? We don't give a flying hoot about your world.

Whenever I need to "get away," I just get away in my mind. I go to my imaginary spot, where the beach is perfect and the weather is perfect. There's only one bad thing there: the flies! They're terrible!

When I think of all the hours and hours of my life I have spent watching television, it makes me realize, Man, I am really rich with television.

Life is a constant battle between the heart and the brain. But guess who wins. The skeleton.

I'm not sure I want to get the nickname "The Love Machine," because how does that affect my nickname now, which is "The Lawn-Cutting Machine"?

If a kid ever asks you how *Santa Claus* can live forever, I think a good answer is that he drinks blood.

They say the mountain holds many secrets, but the biggest is this: "I am a fake mountain."

I don't advocate that children start smoking. But for those kids who already do smoke, boy, it's good, isn't it?

It's funny how two simple words, "I promise," will stall people for a while.

When I think of some of the things that have been done in the name of science, I have to cringe. No, wait, not science, vandalism. And not cringe, laugh.

Instead of a bicycle built for two, what about no kinds of bicycles at all for anybody, anymore? There, are you happy now?

It's too bad cowboys didn't eat much pizza back in the Old West, because I think a good painting would be a cowboy giving his last slice to his horse.

There was probably an old Viking saying that said, "Ax in the head, early to bed; ax in the helmet, a friend of Helmut."

I think it should be a law that if you ever get sucked up into a tornado, whatever you can grab with your hands while you're swirling around up there, you get to keep.

10h/10

Instead of mousetraps, what about baby traps? Not to harm the babies, but just to hold them down until they can be removed.

Isn't it funny how whenever a party seems to be winding down at somebody's house, you can always keep it going just by talking a lot and eating and drinking whatever's left.

I wish somebody would invent a fruit that had no seeds, tasted delicious, and would scream when you ate it.

If you're ever on an airplane that's crashing, see if you can't organize a quick thing of group sex, because come on, you squares.

Toward the end of the Stone Age I bet there was already a feeling that metal was just around the corner.

The king threw back his head and laughed. He enjoyed a good laugh, and so did his wife, the queen. When she saw the king laughing she let out a big laugh too. In fact, she laughed so hard she broke her throne. This made them both laugh harder.

Then they got serious when they remembered they had the plague. "The plague," said the king, but the way he said it made them both burst out laughing again.

To my way of thinking, there's nothing that can't be cured by a big ol' pot of beans. Except maybe bean fever.

When I picked up the little dead mouse that my cat had killed, at first I felt sad. Then I felt hungry. I forget what happened after that.

10/14/10

Once I was passing a roadside fruit stand, and I stopped to ask for directions. There was an old grizzled farmer there, with a face that looked like he had seen many things in his life. I asked him which way to go. He paused for a moment, then took out a handkerchief and wiped his brow. I don't know what he said, because I just peeled out. I don't have time for guys to pull out handkerchiefs.

In the first castles, I bet a common mistake was putting the torture room next to the master bedroom. Boy, you're just not going to get the good sleep that way.

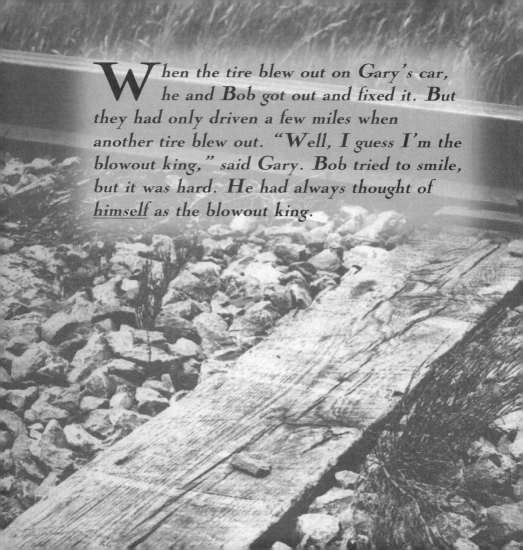

When the tire blew out on Gary's car, he and Bob got out and fixed it. But they had only driven a few miles when another tire blew out. "Well, I guess I'm the blowout king," said Gary. Bob tried to smile, but it was hard. He had always thought of <u>himself</u> as the blowout king.

One time I don't think you should listen to your body is when it says "I'm dead."

I think there is more wisdom in a single drop of rain than there is in all the books in all the libraries of the world. Wait, not rain. Super-concentrated brain juice.

I'd like to see a James Bond movie where James Bond gets behind financially and maybe has to take out a bill consolidation loan, because even when he's applying for the loan he's still real smart-alecky.

Probably one of the worst things about being a genie in a magic lamp is a little thing called "lamp stench."

Instead of a welcome mat, what about just a plain mat and a little loudspeaker that says "welcome" over and over again?

It's funny, but when you look at an old man, then you look at a photo of him when he was a young man, then you look at the old man, then the photo, back and forth, pretty soon you'll do whatever anybody tells you to.

The next time you go to the doctor, go ahead and bring in a stool sample. They might need it. Better go ahead and bring some for the dentist too.

A good way to keep a mob of peasants from killing your monster is when they break into your castle, make them be real quiet, then open a door and there's the monster, sound asleep.

My friend Don is such a loser. But if he was here right now, he'd say I was the loser. No, Don, you're the loser. But if he was here, he'd say I was the loser. No way, Don, you're the loser.

We're all afraid of something. Take my little nephew, for instance. He's afraid of skeletons. He thinks they live in closets and under beds, and at night they come out to get you when you're asleep. And what am I afraid of? Now, I'm afraid of skeletons.

One of the bad things about panning for gold is maybe sometimes you'll get a crawdaddy in your pan, and you start to wonder if you should give up on the gold and just go for crawdaddies. I can't make that decision for you.

When Gary told me he had found Jesus,
I thought, Ya-hoo! We're rich! But
it turned out to be something different.

9/16/10

To become a knife thrower in the circus, they probably don't let you start off throwing at a live woman. They start you out with a little girl.

They were a proud people. In fact, some said they were too proud. If you asked them why they were so proud, they'd just laugh and say, "We're not even going to answer that."

Later, they were tied to the bumper of a car and dragged around the block, as onlookers shrieked with delight. But one old man, who had a banjo, just shook his head and walked away. The crowd noticed this and set him on fire.

I hope I never have to use my underpants as a flag, because after that I could never let my underpants touch the ground.

I f you're being chased by an angry bull, and then you notice you're also being chased by a swarm of bees, it doesn't really change things. Just keep on running.

9/23/10

If they ever have a haunted house for dogs, I think a good display would be a bathtub full of soapy water.

9/9/10

In some countries, what I did would be considered polite, especially Fartland.

When I pick up a handful of sand at the beach and let it dribble through my fingers, I think, Man, this is not a very good vacation.

Police Detective Riley was a no-nonsense kind of guy. Before, he really loved nonsense, and would use it a lot in his murder investigations. But he found that most people didn't appreciate it, especially the family of the victim.

When I saw the old bum pushing his grocery cart down the street, at first I felt sorry for him. But then when I saw what was in his cart I thought, Well, no wonder you're a bum, look at the dumb things you bought.

If they ever build a statue of me, I hope they don't have me with my mouth wide open and holding a sign that says "I love rotten eggs."

1852

CLEARANCE 10 6

Whenever I start thinking that I am not living up to my potential, I remind myself of the old farmer and his fight to the death with the insane pig. It's an exciting story, and it takes my mind off all this "potential" business.

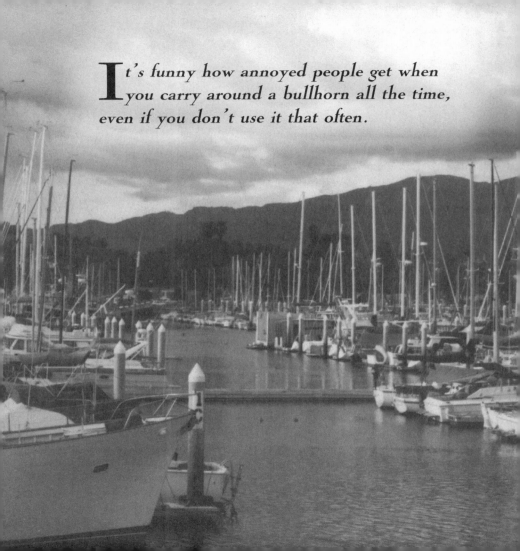

It's funny how annoyed people get when you carry around a bullhorn all the time, even if you don't use it that often.

I'd like to see a movie where a guy is going to die when the sand runs out of an hourglass, but then at the last minute an ant stops the sand from running out. Then the rest of the movie is about the ant.

One of the worst things you can do as an actor, I think, is to forget your lines, and then get so flustered you start stabbing the other actors.

When he was a little boy, he had always wanted to be an acrobat. It looked like so much fun, spinning through the air, flipping, landing on other people's shoulders. Little did he know that when he finally did become an acrobat, it would seem so boring.

Years later, after he finally quit, he found out he hadn't been working as an acrobat after all. He had just been a street weirdo.

Here's a tip: If you ever decide to take apart a bird's nest, to see how it's made, first make sure it's not somebody's basket they got in South America.

I guess if I was starving to death I would eat a dog. But not a collie, because I don't like the taste of collie.

People were always talking about how mean this guy was who lived on our block. But I decided to go see for myself. I went to his door, but he said he wasn't the mean guy, the mean guy lived in that house over there. "No, you stupid idiot," I said, "that's _my_ house."

Y ou might think that the favorite plant of the porcupine is the cactus, but it's thinking like that that has almost ruined this country.

I f you ever get some outer-space guy in a headlock, and his head starts throbbing and glowing different colors, don't let go. That just means the headlock is working.

*S*omeday *I* would like to make a movie that makes people laugh and makes people cry, and then makes them leave the theater in a quick and orderly manner so that others may come in.

A lot of times when you first start out on a project you think, This is never going to be finished. But then it is, and you think, Wow, it wasn't even worth it.

What are all these "other dimensions" I keep hearing about? To me, there's only one dimension worth anything, and that's the good ol' U. S. of A.

I'll never forget the time that skunk got under the house and Grandpa went under to get him. Boy, it smelled for months. You know, that was the last time we ever saw Grandpa.

Whenever you see a bunch of Italian guys talking Italian, just go up to them and start talking fake Italian. They may not understand you exactly, but at least everyone will get a nice warm "Italian" feeling.

4/15/10

Normally I'm not one to believe in little green men from Mars. But one night, as I was driving home from a party, I caught something in my headlights I still can't explain. It had weird, catlike eyes and only stood about a foot tall. It was covered with grayish fur, and walked on all fours, like a cat. It had a tail, which if I had to describe in terms of something here on Earth was, in a way, like a cat's. Also, it was carrying a ray gun in its mouth. It was either a ray gun or a mouse.

I wouldn't mind if animals ate my body, after I'm dead. And before I'm dead, they could lick me.

One day a beaver and a termite were walking down the road together. "I can eat through a tree with my teeth," said the beaver.

"That's nothing," said the termite, "I can burrow through a tree."

Then they heard a voice behind them. "You two think you're so smart, but you're <u>nothing</u>!" It was a bitter old drunk lady.

In my next life, I hope I come back as a parrot, because I already know quite a few words.

If I ever get burned beyond recognition, and you can't decide if it's me or not, just put my funny fisherman's hat on my "head." See, it's me!

When you're dying, a funny gag would be to act like you see an angel, then pretend like you're having sex with it.

Probably one of the main problems with owning a robot is when you want him to go out in the snow to get the paper, he doesn't want to go because it's so cold, so you have to get out your whip and start whipping him, and the kids start crying, and oh why did I ever get this stupid robot?

Warning to all outer-space guys: You can capture me and put me in your "space zoo" if you like, but I will sit way in the back of my cage, where it's hard to see me. And when I do come out, I won't be wearing any pants.

With every new sunrise, there is a new chance. But with every sunset, you blew it.